BRITISH RAIL THROUGH THE 1980s

STEPHEN DANCE

amberley

First published 2023

Amberley Publishing
The Hill, Stroud
Gloucestershire, GL5 4EP

www.amberley-books.com

Copyright © Stephen Dance, 2023

The right of Stephen Dance to be identified as the Author of this work has been asserted in accordance with the Copyrights, Designs and Patents Act 1988.

ISBN 978 1 3981 0562 1 (print)
ISBN 978 1 3981 0563 8 (ebook)

All rights reserved. No part of this book may be reprinted or reproduced or utilised in any form or by any electronic, mechanical or other means, now known or hereafter invented, including photocopying and recording, or in any information storage or retrieval system, without the permission in writing from the Publishers.

British Library Cataloguing in Publication Data.
A catalogue record for this book is available from the British Library.

Orgination by Amberley Publishing.
Printed in the UK.

Contents

Introduction	4
Deltics and the ECML	7
Midland Mainline	14
Western Region	21
Great Eastern Changes	28
Summer Saturdays	34
TransPennine Peak Lament	41
Crompton Cross-country Finale	49
Scottish Loco-hauled Twilight	56
Freight	63
Livery Variations	71
BREL Works	77
Odds and Ends	84
The Mule	90

Introduction

This book is a trip down memory lane as seen through the lens of my camera during the 1980s, with a few photographs that slightly overrun that decade at either end in order to tell the story. The chapters are roughly in chronological order, although some overlap and others cover more or less the whole decade.

By the time the decade opened, the last of the Western Region diesel-hydraulics had been gone for nearly three years and the Deltics were the next class of locomotive to achieve cult status. They had been in decline ever since HSTs started appearing on the East Coast Mainline, but covering their final years was the first major photographic interest I had once I acquired a 35 mm camera. The ECML of the period was full of interest beyond just Deltics though, even after they had gone. 1982, for example, saw one of the most interesting days ever as far as rail traffic is concerned when the Pope visited York in May that year, drawing enthusiasts from all over the country.

Following the end of the Deltics, my next target for the camera was recording the still exclusively locomotive-worked Midland Mainline until the full takeover by HSTs was completed in May 1983. A highlight was photographing and riding on the last locomotive-hauled run of 'The Master Cutler' from Leicester to St Pancras. Very few photographers seemed to take the chance to record the Peaks while they still dominated the line.

Chasing Class 50s featured heavily over the next few years. The refurbishment programme was complete, and we all thought they had many years of service in front of them. Numerous visits were made across the Western Region to record them working. The first withdrawals, within four years of the last refurbished example emerging from Doncaster Works, came as a shock.

As I'd grown up with it as my local line, some time during this period was also taken to cover the Great Eastern Mainline before it was electrified, targeting the infrastructure that would be swept away with modernisation.

Although nowhere near as busy as the 1950s and 1960s, summer Saturdays were still a highlight during the 1980s. Many holiday areas of the country would see large numbers of locomotive-hauled services that dwarfed what was on offer Monday–Friday, many hauled by normally freight-only traction that was spare at weekends, and often by classes not associated with the destination area.

By the middle of the decade British Rail was starting to change radically from the regional structures to business-led sectors. Although sectors had been created from 1982, the only impact they seemed to have in the early years was the introduction of new liveries such as Railfreight and Network SouthEast. From 1987 onwards they began to have a direct effect on railway operation and maintenance. Second generation Sprinter DMUs started to take over formerly locomotive-hauled services, and photographic expeditions started to become one long farewell tour, with locomotive classes disappearing and line after line becoming DMU-only.

The first route to receive Sprinters that attracted my interest were the TransPennine services to/from Scarborough. After they had been replaced on the Midland Mainline, the Class 45/1 Peaks had moved north to dominate the cross-country routes from Liverpool and North Wales to Scarborough and Newcastle, and these were duly covered before Class 150/2 units took over the Scarborough services in May 1987 and the Peaks gave way to Class 47s to/from Newcastle.

Next up to be sprinterised was the Portsmouth–Bristol route, which had been operated by Class 33s since taking over from Class 31s around 1980. Hauling short rakes of Mk 1/2 stock, the Type 3s were ideally suited to this cross-country route, and replacement in May 1988 by Class 155 DMUs could hardly be regarded as an improvement for passengers.

1988 was also the last summer before most of the iconic scenic Scottish lines, such as the Oban, West Highland, Mallaig extension, Kyle of Lochalsh, and Far North, had their locomotive-hauled services replaced with units. I only ever managed the one expedition to Scotland, and quite by chance the weather was largely sunny. Unfortunately RETB signalling between Fort William and Crianlarich had replaced the semaphores on this section only two weeks before I visited.

As a result of sectorisation, the Class 50s lost almost all their InterCity express work and by 1988, outside of summer weekends, passenger work was concentrated on Network SouthEast services in both the Thames Valley from Paddington–Oxford and on the Waterloo–Exeter St Davids route. I'd photographed on the ex-LSWR Mainline many times from 1982 onwards while out chasing Hoovers in the south-west, but now it was rapidly becoming the only reliable place to find them. The class was being rundown; their external and mechanical condition often poor, not helped by lack of further main works visits for overhaul. Laira depot in Plymouth, as with the Westerns in the 1970s, had cared for them for many years, but having to now perform major maintenance tasks, formerly handled at Doncaster Works, such as engine/generator changes wasn't ideal.

The Class 50s disappeared from the Thames Valley in June 1990, and the end of regular services out of Waterloo finally came on 24 May 1992. Class 47s continued until Class 159s DMUs took over, but by July 1993 they had gone too. With most previously locomotive-hauled passenger services now being handled by DMUs, allied with a greatly reduced variety of traction, my interest in UK railways dwindled.

Over the years, many photographs were taken of freight services, but they tended to be bonus shots of trains that passed by while out at a location waiting for some interesting passenger service or other. Information on freight services, particularly up-to-date day-to-day timings, was hard to come by. Books didn't appear until around the mid-1990s, and even then they could only give a general idea of what might be seen at a specific location as many freight services could, and would, run very early, or late, or not at all. Also, some of the most interesting workings were short-term traffic flows, or even one-offs, and printed media simply couldn't keep up; that would have to wait for the internet to become mainstream. Today, of course, we have a plethora of websites accessible from the lineside using smartphones, providing real-time updates of what is running, where it is, and signalling diagrams duplicating what Network Rail staff can see while performing their duties. It's hard to remember that back in the 1980s, as far as freight was concerned, you generally just turned up at the lineside and waited.

Apart from the main livery changes across the decade, such as BR Blue giving way to Large Logo, and then the explosion of business sector colours, many minor and one-off variations appeared. Some were the work of individual depots, others were retro or for special events, but many of the locomotives concerned held celebrity status as a result. A selection of such non-standard liveries is portrayed within this book.

Another area of railway interest that changed greatly during the 1980s were the main railway works. They had been trading as a separate entity, British Rail Engineering Limited, since 1970, but were still responsible for building most new locomotives and rolling stock, performing heavy maintenance and repairs, and disposing of much of BRs redundant assets. Swindon Works closed in 1986, but most of the other main sites survived, until by 1989 BREL had been privatised. The history since then has been complex, but many of the works are now much reduced in scope or closed completely, with most of the historic buildings I have photographed inside of demolished. Only Eastleigh is still anywhere near the size it was in the 1980s, having survived closure in 2006 and reborn as more of an open access engineering facility, able to offer a wide variety of facilities for smaller companies to use.

Finally, a chapter is included of rare workings, railtours, and other miscellaneous images that don't fit in elsewhere.

Mention must be made of the advances, particularly in software, that have made this book possible. Obviously, the photographs published here come from slides and negatives rather than digital images. Some were taken on film that was used because of its price at the time rather than its quality, a decision I've come to regret a great deal over the last forty years. That combined with the inevitable degradation of the actual film over such a long period has made restoration of some images a time-consuming task. Also, films of the period I used were generally a maximum of 200 asa, and sometimes it was tempting to try and use too slow a shutter speed to stop the subject when the light was less than perfect. However, the latest generation of software for sharpening and reducing the effect of film grain has been a revelation. Not only has it transformed some photographs that I had previously dismissed as too difficult to scan into acceptable images, it even has the capability to correct minor speed blurring.

Finally, a big thank you to all the enthusiasts I've had correspondence with over the years on the internet, particularly on Flickr, who have helped identify locomotives, train workings, and even locations where my own notes have gone missing, or provided valuable supporting information for the captions in this book, decades after the events involved.

Deltics and the ECML

55005 *Prince of Wales's Own Regiment of Yorkshire* and 40148 rest in the autumnal sunshine at Haymarket Depot in Edinburgh, 18 October 1980. This was taken during an organised visit for participants on an M&GN Society railtour from Norwich to Edinburgh. Sadly, nowadays, such access is much more difficult, if not impossible to obtain. The Deltic, one of the early casualties, had less than four months left in service, being withdrawn in February 1981.

Nothing sounds like the eighteen-cylinder two-stroke Napier D18-25 engines in a Deltic. 55016 *Gordon Highlander* has just started the second unit and the unique noise is now reverberating around the impressive roof of York station. The locomotive had earlier worked the 09.40 Kings Cross–York and was now preparing to be released from the bay platform. 22 September 1981.

Towards the end of the Deltic era, the timetable at York provided an intriguing opportunity with simultaneous 15.50 departures for Kings Cross and Liverpool. As both started from York, there was more than a chance of catching them together from the footbridge just south of Holgate bridge. Deltics had started appearing on the TransPennine services quite regularly by this time, so there was the possibility of two of the class working side by side (although I've never seen a photograph of that happening). On this occasion, however, 55009 *Alycidon* was on the Kings Cross working, with 40019 *Caronia* heading for Liverpool on 22 September 1981.

55010 *The King's Own Scottish Borderer* ran with only one nameplate for a considerable time before its withdrawal on Christmas Eve 1981, allegedly after damage suffered when someone attempted to remove it. The locomotive is seen here at Grantham awaiting departure with the 15.50 York–Kings Cross on 7 October 1981.

With dawn yet to arrive, brightening skies greet Deltic 55022 *Royal Scots Grey* at Peterborough on 24 October 1981 in charge of the 05.50 Kings Cross–Aberdeen. Having stood here many times over the years during the 1970s and 1980s, I always remember the sickly sweet smell that came from the nearby BSC factory during sugar beet season. Times change; the Deltics have been gone for over forty years, two further generations of ECML motive power have come and nearly gone, and the factory closed in 1991.

55015 *Tulyar* looks immaculate preparing to depart from York with the DPS-organised Deltic Salute railtour, 09.30 York–Aberdeen on 24 October 1981. The Finsbury Park trademark white window surrounds had been reinstated for the previous weekend's Wessex Deltic railtour to Bournemouth. They were removed following the Deltic Salute before appearing for a final time when Tulyar worked the northbound leg of the Deltic Scotsman Farewell special on the final day of the Deltics, 2 January 1982.

Although the Deltics were the main attraction for most enthusiasts visiting the ECML, there was much else of interest to see. Peterborough, for example, was a major hub for parcels traffic, especially in the evenings and overnight. In this picture, 46051 pauses with a northbound working on 9 October 1981.

The lead vehicle appears to be an ex-LMS Full Brake. Up until around this time stock forming parcels trains could be very varied; large numbers of pre-nationalisation vans were still in service, particularly ex-LMS and SR designs. BR abandoned the parcels market during 1981 (with the exception of the Red Star service), and as a result the older stock disappeared very quickly.

55010 *The King's Own Scottish Borderer* and 25250 await their next turn of duty at York MPD on 12 December 1981, one of the coldest days I can remember being out with a camera. 40162 can be seen at the other end of the departmental stock. This picture was taken during an 'unofficial' visit to the depot. With only three weeks left until the end of the Deltics, plenty of other enthusiasts were also taking the same opportunity, and it seemed a Nelson-like blind eye approach was being taken by BR staff.

55016 *Gordon Highlander* waits for the signal at the north end of York station prior to running round having worked the 16.03 Kings Cross–York on the bitterly cold evening of 12 December 1981. In those last few weeks before the end of the Deltics, York became a place of pilgrimage for enthusiasts, at times almost outnumbering normal passengers.

A week later on 19 December 1981 I was back at York, which was bitterly cold again, plus the snow that had gripped the south of England the previous weekend had moved north and east.

In perfect photographic conditions 55002 *The King's Own Yorkshire Light Infantry* is seen backing down onto the 05.10 Plymouth–Scarborough Napier North Eastern railtour. This had been worked from Plymouth to York by 50010 *Monarch*.

55017 *The Durham Light Infantry* is seen unusually in platform 4 at Grantham with the last Deltic-hauled normal service train out of Kings Cross, the 16.03 Kings Cross–York on 31 December 1981.

A broken rail at Barkston Junction, just north of Grantham, put paid to my plan for a last Deltic-hauled trip to Retford and back. Northbound services were queued block on block south of the station and 55017 was sent back south as a special in the path of the 15.50 York–Kings Cross, which was stuck north of Barkston, unfortunately failing en route with the train terminated at Knebworth.

Running some two hours late after being delayed by the broken rail at Barkston Junction, 55015 *Tulyar* awaits departure from Grantham with the 15.50 York–Kings Cross on 31 December 1981. This was the final occasion a Deltic stopped at Grantham during their time in service with BR.

I didn't visit the ECML much after the end of the Deltics, but one very memorable occasion was on 31 May 1982, the day Pope John Paul II visited York. In order to convey the many thousands of visitors, BR organised a huge number of additional and special workings, which also drew enthusiasts from across the country to view the spectacle. Most of the 'Popex' workings at York that day were worked by classes 40, 45, 46, and 47, but a pair of Class 37s were also noted. Of the two I only saw 37068, seen here arriving with the 10.15 Newcastle–York.

The only named Class 46, 46026 *Leicestershire and Derbyshire Yeomanry*, running light engine under Holgate bridge at York, on its way to pick up empty stock to form the 16.27 York–Newcastle additional. 47068 is in the background waiting to work the 16.25 York–Leeds additional on 31 May 1982.

BR did an incredible job that day organising such a mass one-off movement of people from across the country. Even during that era of plentiful summer Saturday locomotive-hauled services it couldn't have been easy finding the resources to provide so many extra workings. The railways of today would not be able to even contemplate such an operation.

Midland Mainline

Screaming through Wellingborough on the Up fast line, 45128 is at the head of the 07.58 Leeds–St Pancras on 29 March 1982. At this time the Midland Mainline was still fully worked by locomotives with hauled stock and dominated by Class 45/1s.

An unidentified Class 45/1 passes Finedon Road Sidings with a St Pancras-bound express and approaches the station at Wellingborough on 29 March 1982. Although empty in this picture, only a few years previously the sidings were busy with freight traffic.

December 1981 saw heavy snowfall over much of Britain, causing transport chaos. 45101 has just arrived at Nottingham Midland and prepares to run round the 09.53 St Pancras–Sheffield on 14 December 1981. For some reason the engine was shutdown, but was unable to be restarted, probably due to flat batteries in the extreme cold.

On a cold, crisp, clear winters day, 45142 roars through Loughborough at close to its 90 mph maximum hauling the 08.00 Sheffield–St Pancras on 18 December 1982.
   The view here has radically changed over the years since 1982 following the extension of the platforms, removal of the sidings, demolition of the signal box and goods shed on the left, as well as major changes to the buildings of the Brush Locomotive Works on the right.

A feature of the Midland Mainline in the East Midlands was the use of pairs of Class 20s on summer dated services to Skegness. Such was the demand for travel that these ran during the week as well as Saturdays during the peak season. 20190 and 20155 are seen here passing through Trent Junction with the 08.20 Leicester–Skegness on 10 August 1982.

A sudden cloudburst has forced me to move under the station canopy at Leicester on a chilly December evening, but the canopy, wet platform and conveniently placed Midland Railway design barrow help make an atmospheric composition, as well as providing somewhere dry to watch 45101 depart with the 16.50 St Pancras–Sheffield on 19 December 1982.

Strong winter sunshine shines directly into the eyes of the driver of 45116 at Sutton Bonington as it rapidly heads south hauling the 09.05 Sheffield–St Pancras on 26 November 1982.

Class 46s were never as common a sight as Class 45s in the East Midlands, but 14 August 1982 found 46027 in the parcels dock at Leicester. Despite its well-worn appearance, the locomotive still had over two years left before withdrawal and is credited as the last Class 46 to run in BR service, when on 26 November 1984 it worked empty stock from Tyne Yard to York and then ran light engine to Doncaster Works where it was switched off for the last time.

45102 calls at Loughborough while working the 10.19 Derby–St Pancras. This section of platform beyond the bridge is no longer publicly accessible. From 4 October 1982 approximately 50 per cent of Midland Mainline services between St Pancras and Sheffield were taken over by HSTs.

Friday 1 October 1982 was the last weekday of full locomotive haulage on the Midland Mainline and therefore the last time a Peak would haul the line's most prestigious service, 'The Master Cutler'. Without any information available in advance I gambled that the headboard would be used, purchased a standard single to St Pancras (off peak tickets were not valid on the Cutler) and waited at Leicester. I wasn't disappointed as 45137 *The Bedfordshire and Hertfordshire Regiment (T.A.)* duly appeared, headboard in place, with the 07.26 Sheffield–St Pancras.

'The Master Cutler' headboard is removed for the last time after 45137s arrival at St Pancras on 1 October 1982. 45148 worked the evening return, but the headboard wasn't used. From the following Monday 'The Master Cutler' was formed of an HST, which are unable to accommodate traditional headboards.

45127 swings left at Trent Junction with the 07.55 St Pancras–Derby on 23 April 1983. Only three weeks remained before the full Midland Mainline HST timetable was introduced on 16 May 1983, after which just two locomotive-hauled weekday peak-hour services each way remained.

The new order at Leicester, 12 October 1982. Less than two weeks after they were introduced to the Midland Mainline, an HST approaches the station past the forest of semaphore signalling with a southbound service for St Pancras.

Western Region

On a perfect winter's day 50023 *Howe* rounds the curve at Venton, just east of Hemerdon Loop, with one of the West of England locomotive-hauled Jumbo services, the 09.40 Paddington–Penzance. These loaded to twelve or more carriages and were introduced to supply extra seating that the fixed formation HSTs couldn't provide. 28 December 1985.

Although Class 50s could be seen on Thames Valley peak-hour stopping services throughout the 1980s right up until they disappeared from the area in 1990, during the early 1980s they could also be seen on off-peak locals too. Slowing for the stop at Pangbourne, 50001 *Dreadnought* is in charge of the 09.25 Oxford–Paddington on 27 August 1982.

50029 *Renown* and 47511 *Thames* arrive simultaneously at Paddington on 7 April 1983. A scene that looks very different today. 50029 is likely to be hauling one of the morning Hereford–Paddington services as they generally included a GUV in the consist. 47511 is probably on an ECS or possibly the Banbury–Paddington via High Wycombe.

The last unrefurbished Hoover, 50014 *Warspite* opens up through the centre road at Reading as it passes non-stop with the 13.22 Oxford–Paddington on 19 March 1983. Within weeks *Warspite* was in Doncaster Works for refurbishment, only to be withdrawn from service less than four years later.

Another scene that has changed out of all recognition several times since the 1970s. Taken from the then relatively new footbridge to the car park at Didcot, 50044 *Exeter* arrives on a fine Sunday evening with the 16.40 Oxford–Paddington on 13 October 1985.

50033 *Glorious* and 47500 *Great Western* on the 08.50 Paddington–Oxford at Appleford on 7 May 1986. This working was often double-headed in order to test locomotives released from maintenance at Old Oak Common. The low platforms at Appleford had recently been replaced, but the pagoda huts survived until around 2005 when they were replaced with glass bus stop-style structures.

45127 provides an unusual sight as it accelerates out of Oxford with the 07.20 Liverpool–Poole on 13 March 1982. Peaks were not everyday sights here, especially on scheduled passenger services, but every so often one would appear, probably with Saltley crews at the controls.

Once a staple traffic source for the railways, newspapers were once delivered every day all over the country by rail. 31120 rounds Crofton curve on a fine sunny Saturday morning with the returning empty vans from Plymouth. 27 August 1983.

Peaks ceased regular West Country operations and were banned west of Bristol after the end of the summer timetable in 1985, ending fifteen years of association with the area. I was therefore surprised to photograph 45125 just west of Hele & Bradninch crossing nearly a year later on 29 August 1986. Many years later, the internet helped identify that the locomotive later worked the 14.53 Exeter St Davids–York relief and that this is probably an ECS positioning move from Malago Vale in Bristol prior to that.

33033 approaches Cowley Bridge Junction with a service from Barnstaple on 25 June 1983. The Cromptons were a common sight around Exeter through much of the 1980s working to Barnstaple, Paignton, and Plymouth, as well as services over the ex-LSWR mainline to Salisbury and beyond.

50028 *Tiger* takes the 10.50 Paddington–Penzance west out of Newton Abbot on 19 June 1983. This scene hasn't so much changed as been completely obliterated. Following the resignalling in 1987 all that remains visible from here is three plain tracks, with everything left of the signal box and right of the locomotive removed.

47054 winds its way round the southern edge of Dartmoor with the Mondays-only 12.30 Paddington–Truro on 20 June 1983. An unusual dated train, this was the last run of the service until it resumed for three weeks on 5–19 September.

A fine evening greets 50044 *Exeter* as it rounds the sharp curve into Par at the head of the 07.44 Dundee–Penzance on 22 June 1983. The train is formed of nine coaches, including a dedicated buffet vehicle and a full brake accommodating bicycles, which were carried for free at the time. Today's railway would have this service formed of a Voyager unit or two, which have nowhere near the same level of facilities or comfort.

A very wet night at Truro finds 47532 with the Up Mail from Penzance to Paddington waiting for loading to be completed on 11 September 1987. A time-honoured working that dated back to the nineteenth century, it came to an end in early January 2004 when the Post Office abandoned Travelling Post Office trains after 166 years.

Great Eastern Changes

47579 *James Nightall* G.C. passes Norwich Thorpe Junction box with a service for Liverpool Street in March 1982. This spot was a favourite summer Saturday haunt for enthusiasts as from here you could see anything using Wensum avoiding curve.

37102 heads south past Dunston with the 11.08 Yarmouth–Liverpool Street on 25 August 1984. Presumably the Class 37 was covering for a failed Class 47/4 as the train is formed of air-conditioned stock.

47579 *James Nightall G.C.* accelerates past Swainsthorpe box and the remains of the station with the 10.17 Norwich–Liverpool Street on 26 August 1984. Despite being closed for thirty years, the station platform and building remained to provide the signalman with water and toilet facilities.

47487 has just passed Wassicks Level Crossing to the north of Haughley Junction while hauling the 16.25 Norwich–Liverpool Street on 26 August 1984. The crossing keeper's house was demolished during the work to electrify the line.

Pre-electrification at Diss as 47574 arrives with the 12.17 Norwich–Liverpool Street on 26 August 1984. The sidings were still in occasional use, served by a trip freight from Ipswich, and the solitary mineral wagon presents a rapidly disappearing, almost bucolic scene.

47574 passes Tivetshall box at speed with the 08.30 Liverpool Street–Norwich on 26 August 1984. Note the signalman's coal supply on the opposite side of the line to the box.

The traditional view of Norwich Thorpe station from Carrow Road bridge as 47573 departs with the 10.32 for Liverpool Street, 25 August 1984. The traction and liveries changed over the years, but this view was more or less unchanged for decades until electrification obliterated most of it.

27 March 1986 and work to simplify and resignal Norwich Thorpe is underway. The signal boxes have been removed and track modifications have started. 45013 is a slightly unusual sight as it departs with a Speedlink freight for Whitemoor yard at March, while 31275 is arriving with a brake van.

Approaching the level crossing at Audley End near Burston, 47566 heads south with the 15.35 Norwich–Liverpool Street on 25 August 1984.

Taken from exactly the same spot as the previous photograph following electrification, 86245 *Dudley Castle* approaches Audley End level crossing with the 14.01 Norwich–Liverpool Street on 25 May 1987.

The post-electrification scene at Tivetshall as 86254 *William Web Ellis* rushes past with the 13.01 Norwich–Liverpool Street on 25 May 1987. One time junction for the long closed Waveney Valley line through Bungay to Beccles, the station finally closed in 1966. The bare area on the right is where the old platform and loop line were located.

On several weekends in the early part of 1986 Norwich station was closed to allow track rationalisation and resignalling ready for the forthcoming electrification. In order to provide some kind of service for passengers, the closed but still extant station at Trowse was temporarily reopened, with some of the Liverpool Street workings running to/from Yarmouth via the Wensum avoiding curve. In this shot we see 31417 arriving from Crown Point with the 15.30 Norwich–Liverpool Street. A Metro Cammell Class 101 unit awaits departure to Lowestoft in the adjacent platform.

Summer Saturdays

Class 47/3s were not common motive power for the 09.45 Paddington–Newquay, but 16 June 1984 found 47326 in charge, seen here climbing the steep gradient of the Luxulyan Valley just below the Treffry viaduct.

31114 passes Intwood Crossing near Norwich with the 13.38 Yarmouth–Birmingham New Street on 31 July 1982. The locomotive had earlier worked into Norwich along with 31126 on the 08.04 Birmingham New Street–Yarmouth, but after 37053 failed on 10.52 Liverpool Street–Yarmouth, 31126 was borrowed to cover for that, leaving 31114 to haul ten coaches back to the West Midlands on its own. According to comments received from an enthusiast on board that day, performance was quite lively for a single Type 2 locomotive on such a heavy load.

Winding along the sea wall on the approaches to Teignmouth, 50042 *Triumph* is at the head of the 11.33 Manchester–Newquay on 18 June 1983.

47075 emerges from Whiteball tunnel with the 08.00 Swansea–Penzance on 25 June 1983.
    The locomotive is still in late 1970s condition with domino headcode panel and no headlight. However, some six weeks later I photographed it again at Norwich, and by then the headcode panel had become yellow, with a headlight fitted by the following April.

Large Logo-liveried 47450 heads for Norwich at Cantley with a Saturday afternoon ECS movement on 23 August 1986. The industrial infrastructure in the background at this rural outpost is the BSC sugar factory, which in years past used to receive much rail traffic.

45131 storms through Dawlish Warren in the early evening of 18 June 1983, another glorious summer Saturday, working hard on the 17.25 Paignton–York.

An enthusiast enjoys both locomotives working hard as 31102 and 31245 ascend Hethersett bank with the 14.44 Yarmouth–Derby on 31 July 1982. This used to be a quiet rural location, but is now right alongside the rerouted dual carriageway A11, with the level crossing in the background replaced by an overbridge.

46037 descends from Whiteball summit with the 08.26 Bradford–Paignton on 25 June 1983.
  This locomotive ended its career on 16 June 1984, catching fire while climbing the Lickey Bank with the 10.35 Penzance–Leeds. I nearly got a shot of this working as it passed by a few miles away while I was photographing on the Newquay branch (including 47326 from earlier in this chapter).

Seen from the wonderful viewpoint of the Treffry viaduct, 45125 descends the Luxulyan valley with the 08.55 Newquay–Manchester on 16 June 1984. Through trains to/from the major conurbations during holiday season had been a feature of Cornish resort branch lines for decades, but by 1984 only the line to Newquay still hosted such services. Although not altogether abandoned, services were severely curtailed and locomotives effectively banned after the summer season of 1987 when the manual signalling and run round facilities at Newquay were removed.

The leading coach has a full complement of enthusiasts enjoying haulage by 46047, which is working the 07.28 Leeds–Newquay as it nears Dawlish on 18 June 1983. Window hanging along the sea wall was always one of life's great pleasures, now sadly impossible with almost all opening window fitted stock eliminated or strictly monitored.

40080 moves slowly out of the platform at Norwich having worked in on the 08.15 Manchester–Yarmouth on 6 August 1983. Class 40s had appeared sporadically at Norwich on this summer Saturday working for years, but during the 1983 season they became a regular, weekly feature. Unfortunately this wasn't repeated in 1984 as withdrawals reduced Class 40 numbers. 40080 only lasted another month or so, until 12 September 1983.

The classic viewpoint at Parsons tunnel as 47497 emerges back into the sunshine with the 08.36 Cardiff–Paignton on 9 June 1984. The size of the rocks forming the sea defences compared to the locomotive show what a challenge it is keeping this section of line operational.

46018 climbs towards Whiteball tunnel on 25 June 1983 with what is believed to be the 09.50 Newquay–Newcastle, as the locomotive had worked down the previous evening with the 21.17 Newcastle–Newquay. Although much less busy on summer Saturdays than in the 1950s, during the several hours spent here that day, a train was signalled in one direction or the other throughout that period.

47512 passes Dawlish Warren on the through road at the head of the 14.10 Paddington–Paignton on 18 June 1983. What better way to end a day on the sea wall, listening to the block bells and observing the signalman at work. The box became redundant from 14 November 1986 when this section of line was resignalled, and was demolished in 1990.

TransPennine Peak Lament

45136 sits under the magnificent roof at York as it pauses with the 08.46 Liverpool–Scarborough on 7 September 1986. A view that had changed little since the days of steam was on borrowed time – electrification would soon despoil the scene, and the centre roads removed.

45118 *The Royal Artilleryman* arrives at York with the 15.29 Scarborough–Liverpool on 7 September 1986. In common with many of the named Peaks around this time, the nameplates have been removed; the bolts can still be seen to the right of the grill.

45118 *The Royal Artilleryman* emerges from Standedge Tunnel at Diggle with the 07.10 Newcastle–Liverpool on 5 September 1986. This locomotive is now preserved.

45144 *Royal Signals* winds its way alongside the River Derwent at Low Hutton with the 09.03 Liverpool–Scarborough on 6 September 1986.

45103 reverses out of the platform at Scarborough having arrived with the 14.03 from Liverpool on 6 September 1986. I missed out on capturing the full semaphore signalling here as the track layout had been simplified the year before. Locomotive-hauled services have returned to Scarborough in recent years in the form of Class 68s.

45150 nears the top of the climb to Standedge tunnel past the loop and semaphores at Diggle with the 09.03 Liverpool–Scarborough on 5 September 1986.

A sunny day at Mirfield finds 47489 bound for Holyhead with the 10.53 from Scarborough on 5 September 1986. Peaks dominated at this time on TransPennine services, but some Class 47s were diagrammed too.

45130 crosses the double-deck High Level Bridge at Newcastle with ECS to form the 16.17 to Liverpool on 20 September 1986. This was captured from the top of Newcastle castle keep.

Evening sunshine highlights 45106 as it passes the signal box at Marsden with the 15.53 Scarborough–Liverpool on 3 September 1986. This locomotive was one of the final class survivors. Withdrawn on 27 July 1988, it was then reinstated on 4 August 1988 and painted green. It was finally withdrawn after catching fire on the 07.12 Derby–St Pancras on 3 February 1989.

45130 catches a patch of sunshine amid the shadows at Newcastle as it removes empty stock off the 06.10 from Liverpool on 20 September 1986.

The classic view from under Holgate bridge just south of York station. 45136 is in charge of the 15.29 Scarborough–Liverpool on 7 September 1986. The area around and under Holgate bridge was easily accessible at this time; plenty of enthusiasts and photographers took advantage of that.

47522 exits Standedge tunnel with the 14.03 Liverpool-Scarborough on 3 September 1986. The following year the locomotive was repainted apple green and named *Doncaster Enterprise*. Four tunnels run side by side here, the active railway bore, two disused single track railway bores to the left, and the Huddersfield Narrow Canal bore, the entrance of which is out of sight.

45130 slowly brings empty coaching stock into Newcastle along the ECML from the Heaton direction on 20 September 1986.

Crompton Cross-country Finale

33027 *Earl Mountbatten of Burma* is seen at Hindon Road crossing near Wylye hauling the 14.00 Cardiff–Portsmouth on 3 March 1988. The SR two digit headcode for services on the Portsmouth Harbour–Bristol route was 89. 79 was usually used if Portsmouth & Southsea was the starting point or destination.

33049 approaches Dunbridge at the head of the 12.10 Portsmouth–Cardiff on 3 March 1988. The Type 3 Cromptons with 1550 hp on tap were ideally suited to these light cross-country services.

Several workings on the core cross-country route from Portsmouth to Bristol were formed of longer distance services. Here we see 33018 at Bristol Temple Meads in charge of the 08.20 Brighton–Cardiff, while Peak 45038 departs with the 10.00 Paignton–Liverpool on 11 August 1984.

An Ivo Peters inspired location by the River Avon at Bradford-on-Avon, which I believe is no longer accessible due to residential development. One of the original WR named Class 47s, 47564 *Colossus*, passes by with the 12.10 Portsmouth–Cardiff on 23 April 1988. Class 47s appeared on the route from time to time.

With the village of Bathford in the background, and the Kennet and Avon Canal clinging to the hillside, 33065 has just traversed Bathampton Junction and entered the Avon valley on a beautiful spring evening with the 16.20 Cardiff–Portsmouth. 23 April 1988.

What appears to be a peaceful rural scene is anything but, as the M27 motorway is 200 yards behind the photographer, nearly drowning out the sound of the approaching Crompton. 33026 is Southampton-bound near the site of the former station at Nursling with the 13.05 Cardiff–Portsmouth Harbour on 6 August 1987.

33012 exits the short tunnel having just restarted the 13.05 Cardiff–Portsmouth away from its stop at Bradford-on-Avon on 23 April 1988. The Class 33s were in their last few weeks of service on this route and were about to be replaced with what proved to be the less than successful Class 155 DMUs.

33020 catches the evening sunshine as it sweeps north through the Avon valley while working the 16.10 Portsmouth-Bristol on 23 April 1988.

A gorgeous spring day at Bradford-on-Avon as Class 33/2 Slim Jim 33208 accelerates away from the station at the head of the 13.10 Portsmouth–Bristol on 11 May 1988. Since the most restricted tunnels on the Hastings line had had clearances eased by being singled during electrification work in 1986, the Class 33/2s, built to that line's slimmer loading gauge, were no longer required to work traffic on that route. They could now be found anywhere Class 33s roamed.

Another Ivo Peters classic location, Claverton Weir. 33039 passes by in charge of the 08.30 Brighton–Cardiff on 11 May 1988.

Push-pull fitted 33114 brings the 15.10 Portsmouth–Cardiff around the curve at Freshford on a beautiful spring afternoon, 23 April 1988. A location still much used by photographers today.

33059 near Norton Bavant with the 13.05 Cardiff–Portsmouth as 47368 heads north with a short Speedlink working on 15 June 1987. The freight is formed of what appears to be a ferry van, a VEA modernised Vanwide, and a VDA van, so may be destined for Warminster with MoD traffic.

The last week of locomotive-hauled services through the Avon valley near Bath and 33009 is seen passing the diminutive Avoncliff Halt with the 12.10 Portsmouth–Cardiff on 11 May 1988. The halt previously had wooden shelters on both platforms. The left-hand one was destroyed during the great storm of October 1987, but has since been replaced with one in the same style.

33026 approaches Freshford station with the 16.15 Bristol–Portsmouth on the afternoon of 23 April 1988. The Class 155 DMUs that replaced the locomotive-hauled services a few weeks later proved to be less than reliable, with reports of doors opening while on the move causing them to be withdrawn and replaced with Class 156s. Most were eventually rebuilt into single car form as Class 153s.

Scottish Loco-hauled Twilight

37406 *The Saltire Society* waits at Arrochar and Tarbet with the 10.04 Glasgow–Fort William for 37413 to arrive from the north with the 08.40 Fort William–Glasgow on 14 June 1988. Having arrived here under grey, overcast skies I wasn't hopeful of a great photograph, but the weather changed to cloudless blue overhead within about ten minutes.

Late evening at Inverness finds 47469 *Glasgow Chamber of Commerce* and 47356 stabled and awaiting their next duties on 14 June 1988. 47469 wears ScotRail branded InterCity Executive colours, while 47356 is adorned in the earlier version of Railfreight grey for 47s, without the later red stripe along the lower bodyside.

37410 *Aluminium 100* approaches the Pass of Brander at Bridge of Awe with the 08.10 Oban–Glasgow on 18 June 1988. Note the semaphore signal here and the apparatus across the track opposite. This section of line is very prone to rockfalls and is lined with cables alongside the track. If a fall occurs, the disturbance to the cables triggers the device and causes the signal to be set to danger. The system is known as Anderson's Piano.

47430 arrives at Pitlochry hauling the 12.30 Inverness–Glasgow. 37049 *Imperial* waits by the signal box for access to the single-track section while working light engine towards Inverness. 18 June 1988.

37417 *Highland Region* enters Muir of Ord station with the 05.58 Wick/Thurso–Inverness on 15 June 1988. The signal box still survived at the time and was manned, despite the semaphores having recently been removed following introduction of RETB signalling between Dingwall and Inverness. The armless signal posts can be seen in the background.

47577 heads south with The Clansman 10.35 Inverness–Euston in the scenic Pass of Killiecrankie at Garry Bridge, just north of Pitlochry, on 18 June 1988.

37423 *Sir Murray Morrison 1873–1948* at the head of the Royal Scotsman land cruise train as it takes the line to Oban through Strath Fillan near Crianlarich on 14 June 1988. The locomotive had only been named for less than a month and was still looking smart in its new triple grey Metals and Automotive sector Railfreight livery.

37421 waits at Kyle of Lochalsh with the 16.40 to Inverness on 15 June 1988. The first vehicle is an ex-Class 101 Metro Cammell Driving Trailer that has been converted into an observation car. This was used on the 10.15 from Inverness and the 16.40 return, which was named 'The Hebridean'. Although the line was taken over by Sprinters from April 1989, this service survived as loco-hauled until 1995.

One of the most spectacular locations on Britain's railways. 37405 *Strathclyde Region* approaches County March Summit north of Crianlarich with the very late running 14.45 Fort William–Glasgow on 14 June 1988. The section of line from Crianlarich to Fort William had only commenced RETB signalling operation a couple of weeks previously on 28 May 1988 and presumably the system was still having a few problems.

Climbing the final few hundred yards to County March Summit, 37408 *Loch Rannoch* is in charge of the daily Mossend–Fort William Speedlink freight service on 14 June 1988.

37409 *Loch Awe* drifts past the signal box at Mallaig Junction, Fort William, with the 18.45 Mallaig–Fort William on 15 June 1988. Semaphores survived here despite both the lines to Mallaig and Crianlarich having been converted to RETB signalling.

A classic Mallaig line location is Loch nan Uamh viaduct, and in this shot 37406 *The Saltire Society* crosses with the 15.55 Mallaig–Fort William on 16 June 1988.

37406 *The Saltire Society* crosses the causeway at the eastern end of Loch Dubh near Polnish with the 12.30 Mallaig–Fort William on 16 June 1988.

47468 passes Blackford level crossing and signal box with the 16.35 Inverness–Glasgow on 18 June 1988. Scotland lost most of its internal locomotive-hauled passenger services very quickly. The West Highland, Mallaig and Oban lines suffered Class 156s from January 1989, with the Far North and Kyle lines following in April. Class 158s entered squadron service through 1989, taking over services to Inverness and Aberdeen as well as Glasgow–Edinburgh. By 1992, Scotland no longer had an allocation of Class 47s.

Freight

20177 and 20113 take a loaded train of 21-ton coal hoppers and mineral wagons east through Nottingham Midland during March 1982, possibly destined for Staythorpe A power station near Newark, which closed in October 1983. Much of the traditional coal traffic such as this disappeared very quickly after the miners strike of 1984/5. Already in decline, many 16-ton mineral wagons were damaged after standing loaded for weeks during the strike, and their numbers plummeted as the coal industry was cut back.

Class 13 only had three members, formed of two Class 08s modified as master and slave units for hump shunting in Tinsley Yard. Here we see 13003 propelling a rake of wagons over the hump on 3 July 1981. The overhead catenary was part of the 1,500 volt DC electrified Woodhead route to Manchester, closure of which was only some two weeks away. By this time use of the hump was in serious decline, and hump shunting ceased altogether in 1984.

45043 *The Kings Own Royal Border Regiment* begins the descent of Dainton bank towards Totnes past the tiny hamlet of Wrigwell with an engineers/departmental working on 8 June 1984.

The first wagons are vintage 1950s/60s opens, the first a Highfit and the second a Shock High, loaded with what appears to be scrapped wheelsets. The second wagon is marked 'Return to AME Cathays Cardiff'.

I don't know if the second man is observing the train as it starts down the steep bank, or checking us out on the bridge.

Another bastion of traditional, steam era freight stock in the 1980s was China Clay traffic. Newer air-braked stock had already taken over the long distance traffic flows, but the 13-ton, wooden-bodied, 9-foot wheelbase Clayhoods still survived for local traffic within Cornwall until replaced by CDA wagons based on the MGR coal hopper design from 1987. Here we see 37175 having positioned a rake of Clayhoods in Moorswater Clay Dries on 1 September 1986.

Seen at Aldermaston on 26 August 1983, 47060 takes a rake of empty 27-ton iron ore tipplers, now in use on aggregates traffic, slowly westwards, back to the Mendip quarries. From 1970, Foster Yeoman, and then ARC started using rail as their primary means of transporting stone to their customers from Merehead and Whatley. BR vacuum-braked hoppers, mineral wagons and tipplers were initially used to carry this traffic. Often overloaded, wagon failures and derailments lead to new, privately owned fleets of air-braked wagons being deployed from 1972 onward. The ex-iron ore tipplers seen here didn't last on these workings much longer.

Taken from the bridge abutment of the abandoned MSWJR line at Wolfhall, 47014 winds its way round the reverse curves with a rake of empty, four-wheeled, air-braked hoppers bound for Whatley quarry on 3 August 1985. The wagons shown here were introduced from around 1974 onwards, to a number of slightly different designs under the TOPS code PGA.

The highly unusual sight of 56050, 56048 and 47901 at Wolfhall with aggregate empties heading towards Westbury on 28 September 1985. I don't know if this was because of a failure, or if one or more locomotives were hitching a lift back to the Mendips. Today, seeing multiple locomotives being conveyed dead in tow is a familiar sight in order to save a timetable path, and therefore money, but triple-heading on these workings back in the 1980s was very rare. From the early 1980s onwards, high capacity bogie box wagons started appearing on traffic from both Merehead and Whatley.

Only about three months old, 59003 takes a load of Mendip stone eastwards past Wolfhall on 2 May 1986. After many years working in Germany, 59003 returned to the UK in 2014 and is now owned by GBRf. Still a familiar sight today, the Class 59s transformed the Mendips aggregates traffic, being able to handle 4,000-ton trains single-handed and being exceptionally reliable. The same can't be said of these wagons. This batch of PHA bogie hoppers were built in 1984 from aluminium, which proved to not be strong enough for the payload and the bodies were scrapped around 1989.

Cement is still carried by rail today, but not in these four-wheeled Presflo wagons. 47087 *Cyclops* passes Cowley Bridge Junction with what is probably a Westbury–Exeter Central working on 11 June 1984.

Different generations of motive power at Oxford on 7 June 1985. 45063 waits on the centre road with a southbound Speedlink working, as 58023 takes MGR coal empties north from Didcot Power Station.

56078 takes northbound MGR coal empties from Didcot Power Station up Hatton Bank on a fine spring evening on 6 May 1988. Although Class 56s were still regular visitors to Didcot Power Station, Class 58s tended to dominate traffic to/from Didcot by the late 1980s. Coal was the main reason that railways were built in the first place, but nearly 200 years later, only a soon to be extinguished trickle of such traffic remains.

31217 is seen at Colton South Junction with Speedlink working 6L91, Hull Speedlink Yard–York Dringhouses, on 5 September 1986. On this working the ferry van would be going from Hull King George Dock back to Dover having brought paper products into Hull; the tanks are from BP Chemicals at Saltend, carrying various chemicals going to Haverton Hill, Seal Sands, Dalry, Powfoot, Plumpton Junction, and Sellafield. 6L91 was routed via Gilberdyke, Goole and Ferrybridge to allow traffic to be picked up at Goole, which at this time included imported cars and some bulk grain. Such complex itineraries were operationally expensive, and after sectorisation it was concluded that most wagon load traffic in the UK simply couldn't make money, and was abandoned in 1991. Despite several attempts since then to revive wagon load services, all have been unsuccessful.

Unrefurbished 31196 leads refurbished 31304 past Mirfield with a Preston Docks–Lindsey empty tanks working on 5 September 1986. The first six tanks are for bitumen traffic. This service survives today, but now only conveys bitumen. The number of refineries and distribution depots has markedly reduced since the 1980s, but most of the survivors are still rail served, except where pipelines handle deliveries.

With a spectacular backdrop of the Trossachs, 37401 *Mary Queen of Scots* heads west up Strath Fillan on the Oban line near Crianlarich with a rake of TTA tanks forming the thrice-weekly freight from Glasgow to Oban on 17 June 1988. The service principally conveyed fuel to the depot at Connel Ferry and ceased in 1993.

37408 *Loch Rannoch* shunts timber wagons in Crianlarich Lower Yard on 17 June 1988 at the site of the former Callander and Oban line station closed in September 1965. The West Highland line viaduct can be seen crossing in the background. 37408 had worked from Oban with empty fuel tanks, left them on the former Callander and Oban stub at Lower Crianlarich Junction (where the line climbs up to the West Highland station), before running light engine into the yard to collect timber wagons. Crianlarich Lower Yard closed in 1993 with just 400 yards of track left as a siding at Lower Crianlarich Junction.

Livery Variations

Stratford TMD kicked off the trend for depot special liveries in 1977 when 47163 and 47164 were repainted for the Silver Jubilee with silver roofs and large bodyside Union Jacks. This eventually morphed into standard Stratford trim, which is seen here with rail grey roof. 47579 *James Nightall G.C.* passes the disused platforms at Trowse with a Liverpool Street-bound working on 29 May 1982.

In 1979 45121 and 45110 had white stripes painted on their lower bodysides and cantrails in the style of their original green livery. 45114 had a grey roof applied, and later possibly bodyside stripes too. These were all removed sometime in 1981. 45121 is seen at Derby preparing to work the 14.07 to St Pancras on 22 July 1981.

The Finsbury Park-allocated Deltics had white cab window surrounds applied in 1979 as a morale booster for staff as the depot started to be rundown after the introduction of HSTs on the ECML. When the racehorse named Deltics were allocated away from FP, the surrounds were painted back into blue, only reappearing on 55015 in October 1981 for a pair of railtours, and then again for the final day, 2 January 1982. 55018 *Ballymoss* rests on Haymarket depot in Edinburgh on 18 October 1980.

Several Class 33/1s had their window surrounds painted white from 1982 to around 1984. At least 33101, 33105, 33107, and 33119 are known to have been so treated. 33101 is on the rear of the 15.10 Salisbury–Waterloo as it accelerates away from Whitchurch on 25 August 1982.

D200, or 40122 if you prefer, was the first of the Class 40s and became a celebrity locomotive for the last few years before withdrawal and preservation. Originally withdrawn on 23 August 1981 after some weeks out of service, then reinstated on 24 April 1983, Toton depot restored her and she re-entered traffic on 31 July 1983 repainted in green with full yellow ends. Final withdrawal into preservation was on 18 April 1988, two days after working her final railtour from Liverpool Street to Norwich and then onto York. Here we see D200 on display at Crown Point Open Day at Norwich on 24 September 1983.

Several Large Logo-liveried Class 50s had black roofs applied, but only one, to my knowledge, ever had the roof painted blue and that was 50010 *Monarch* during the summer of 1983. The repaint took place at Landore depot in Swansea, and apparently they had run out of grey paint, so improvised. In this shot, 50010 is in charge of the 07.40 Penzance–Liverpool approaching Aller Junction on 29 August 1983.

31135 ran for some years with a unique livery variation after receiving a depot repaint at Old Oak Common in 1982. It had Hymek-style extended yellow cabside window surrounds applied. On 15 June 1985 31135 was in charge of the returning empty newspaper vans from Plymouth, seen here near Crofton.

A number of Class 31/4s received bodyside stripes. Those from ER had white stripes, while the WR examples so treated had rail grey. ER 31413 takes the 10.30 Birmingham New Street–Yarmouth past the level crossing and signal box at Buckenham on 23 August 1986.

As part of the GW150 celebrations, four Class 47s and a Class 50 were repainted into lined Brunswick Green from 1984 onwards. 50007 *Hercules* was also renamed *Sir Edward Elgar* and can be seen here at Radley with the 16.25 Oxford–Paddington on 14 April 1985.

47628 *Sir Daniel Gooch* accelerates the 12.03 Poole–Newcastle away from a signal stop at Moreton Cutting near Didcot on 7 February 1989. Still in GW150 colours, four years after the event, by April 1990 47628 had been repainted into InterCity Executive livery and lost its name and numberplates.

33008 *Eastleigh* was repainted into green livery in 1986, initially in simplified form with full yellow ends and no stripe. The stripe was quickly added, and by August that year, the white window surrounds were applied, with full retro treatment of the cab ends completed by early 1987. 33008 is seen here at Avoncliff hauling the 13.05 Cardiff–Portsmouth on 11 May 1988.

56019 had, I believe, a unique variation on Railfreight Grey Red Stripe livery when in 1988 it was repainted in that livery, but with red bufferbeams plus cowling and even received red buffers. Only a few days after the repaint following maintenance at Crewe Works, on 6 May 1988 it came to the rescue of failed 31409 at Banbury on the 12.38 Poole–Manchester and is seen here in Harbury cutting.

BREL Works

Derby Works open day on 4 September 1982 and the scrapyard is obviously a big draw for enthusiasts. Present here (L–R) are 25105, 25066, and prototype HST power car 41001 (now preserved). Obviously public events back then were far more relaxed safety wise than today. A modern Health & Safety inspector would be speechless.

27014 and 27104 are inspected by young enthusiasts at Derby Works open day on 4 September 1982. 27014 has a chalked inscription on the cab door: 'Warning, Keep Off, Blue Asbestos'. I doubt the public would even be allowed inside the building today, should an event such as this even be allowed.

Back in the days when what were effectively the railways own workshops still designed and built locomotives. 58016/7/8 are under construction at Doncaster Works on 28 July 1984. The lines between the roles of the larger traction maintenance depots and BREL works became ever more blurred following sectorisation, and eventually shattered after privatisation. Most ex-BREL works today are either much reduced in size and scope, or closed altogether.

As well as heavy maintenance, the main works would also undertake modification programmes. One of the major schemes during the 1980s was the refurbishment of the Class 50s at Doncaster, which took about four years to complete. Here, work is progressing on 50028 *Tiger*, on 13 June 1982, with new bodywork panels welded in and primed as well as the bodywork modifications underway for fitting the headlight, replacement of the air filtration system, and removal of the sandbox fillers. Brand new 56108 and 31137 receiving collision repairs are the locomotives in the background.

Another major role undertaken by BREL Works was the melancholy task of disposing of redundant locomotives and rolling stock. 46038 meets its end in the scrap yard at Swindon Works, 30 August 1985, having been withdrawn on 28 March 1982 following a main generator failure.

Not even 'ex' works, 50001 *Dreadnought* gleams in the sun at Doncaster Works on 28 July 1984 following the open day. The locomotive had just emerged from the paint shop in Large Logo livery, and had yet to turn a wheel in service after a general overhaul, its first since refurbishment.

An overhead view of the main shop at Doncaster Works after the open day on 28 July 1984, taken from the crane access ladder. The Class 50s on view are, at the front, 50041 *Bulwark* being repaired after its accident on the Penzance sleepers at Paddington on 23 November 1983; behind it is 50013 *Agincourt*, the last standard BR blue 50 left, which would emerge in Large Logo livery. At the back on the right is 50033 *Glorious* and in front of it 50020 *Revenge*. 37100 and 37133 are alongside 50041. 31412 and 31307 are also present.

Not much is left of 40141 as cutting is nearly complete at Doncaster Works on 28 July 1984. The Spanner steam heating boiler is still in situ, just behind the remains of the cab.

Class 42 Warship D818 *Glory* sits alongside the main line at Swindon Works on 30 August 1985. Withdrawn from service on 31 October 1972, *Glory* arrived at Swindon on 26 April 1973 and was used as a source of spares for D832 *Onslaught*, which had been claimed for further use by Derby Research Centre. It became a gatekeeper for the works, often on display around the turntable, and was repainted as an apprentice exercise at least twice over the years. By the time this photograph was taken, the locomotive was in poor external condition, internally little more than a shell, and was cut up for scrap less than two months later. With the then recent announcement of the closure of Swindon Works, there are conflicting accounts for the reason behind the scrapping, but *Glory*'s final legacy was to yield spares to aid in the preservation of D821 *Greyhound* and D832 *Onslaught*.

25139, 25115 and 25101 await their fate next to the turntable at Swindon Works on 30 August 1985. The turntable is a listed structure and still exists in situ.

40140 at Derby Works on 4 September 1982. Withdrawn on 7 March 1982, 40140 was yielding spares to keep other class members in service. It was scrapped at Crewe Works in August 1983.

45145 and 45117 outside the Test House at Derby Works during the open day on 4 September 1982.

Push-pull fitted Class 47/7 47709 *The Lord Provost* looks nearly ready to re-enter traffic after overhaul at Crewe Works during an organised Saturday visit on 12 March 1983.

45009 is undergoing overhaul at Crewe Works on 12 March 1983. Presumably its last major classified repair, it lasted only another three years, being withdrawn in March 1986.

Odds and Ends

A Class 103 Park Royal DMU leaves Crewe in late July or early August 1978. Taken with my Kodak Instamatic, I somehow managed to get both the shot framed correctly and achieved a blur-free image; no mean feat with an Instamatic when photographing a moving subject. Only twenty Park Royal sets were built – they suffered badly from corrosion, and by 1978 around half had been withdrawn with the survivors all allocated to Chester, which probably accounts for why I took a DMU picture. All were out of service by February 1983.

Sundays at Birmingham New Street often provided the opportunity for haulage by freight locomotives when the overhead power supply was off for maintenance, or line closures forced diversion of Birmingham services via Nuneaton over non-electrified track. 28 March 1982 was one such Sunday drag, and 56101 is in charge of the 09.40 Euston–Wolverhampton, which it took over from an electric locomotive at Nuneaton.

40084 and 40057 pass through the centre road at Oxford with the York–Paddington Cotswold Venturer railtour on 8 May 1982. A thirty-minute spell on the footbridge here had produced this railtour, 45033 on a Sheffield–Reading additional, the more normal sight of 50039 *Implacable* on the 13.55 Oxford–Paddington, and then 37177 turned up with the 11.35 Poole–Newcastle. Although the railtour had been known about in advance, you just never knew what was going to appear in those pre-internet days.

25191 shunts a very unusual load into the GWS premises at Didcot on 12 May 1986. The train is conveying the replica broad gauge 4-2-2 *Iron Duke*. Doubly rare, as apart from being a one-off event, Class 25s were very thin on the ground on WR metals by this time.

Regular, but not common visitors to the Thames Valley on freight during the early 1980s, Class 25s on passenger workings were most unusual, and singletons very rare. 25175 plods down the relief line at Cholsey on a spring evening, with what was eventually identified, years later, as an 18.05 Reading–Altrincham return excursion. 30 April 1983.

Although, as already noted in this book, Peaks were seen at Oxford and Reading from time to time on cross-country services, appearances at Paddington were far less frequent. An exception to this occurred for a few months around the beginning of 1984 when a Class 45/1 was actually diagrammed to work the 09.35 Cardiff–Paddington, returning on the 13.07 Paddington–Liverpool. Unlike some diagrams that never seemed to produce the advertised locomotives, Peaks worked this one quite regularly for a while. 45117 approaches Reading with the 13.07 Paddington–Liverpool on 25 January 1984.

An unusual load at Salisbury behind 33001 on 14 April 1984. The Crompton is at the head of the exhibition train promoting Welsh narrow gauge railways, including Talyllyn Railway No. 3 *Sir Haydn* (ex-Corris Railway) loaded on a Flatrol wagon. Note the piece of old carpet protecting the paintwork from the chains attaching the loco to the wagon. Another item of interest is that the exhibition coach carries its number on the solebar. Being in exhibition use meant frequent repainting to suit whatever purpose it was hired for.

33109 runs round the boat train at Weymouth Quay, which had arrived from Waterloo shortly before, on 24 August 1982. Scheduled public services on the fascinating tramway section through the streets of Weymouth ceased on 26 September 1987. Sporadic railtours traversed the line until the last train ran on 2 May 1999. The track was left intact after the last railtour for over twenty years until work to remove the rails commenced in 2020.

A pair of Choppers at Dawlish was not an everyday sight. 20124 and 20094 take the Chopper Topper II railtour from Wolverhampton to Penzance along the sea wall on 31 August 1986. This tour included a trip over the freight-only branch from Burngullow to Parkandillack.

A bitterly cold morning shows to good effect that the steam heat boiler on the Class 46 is in full operational order, and helps enhance a photograph of the undeniably ugly concrete cavern that is Birmingham New Street; a place that was hard to avoid when travelling by rail from the East Midlands to anywhere where Class 50s could be found. 45146 is on the 06.02 Sheffield–Cardiff while 46051 is preparing to work the 08.15 Birmingham New Street–Plymouth on 13 March 1982.

Whatever 37193, 37199 and 37240 are working is a complete mystery as they head west at Basildon on 13 May 1988 with a short rake of empty MGR hoppers. Too short to be a genuine MGR working, maybe the wagons are being returned from repair, possibly from Stratford or Eastleigh?

45034 lifts a heavy stone train out of Peak Dale through the sheer rock cutting towards Doveholes tunnel on 4 September 1986. This shot was a close run thing, having spotted 45034 from the car leaving Peak Dale. A quick dash up the road, and a sprint across the field adjoining the line brought us to the edge of the cutting just as the Peak, working hard, came round the corner.

The Mule

50047 *Swiftsure* runs into Basingstoke on a cold winters morning with the 05.45 Plymouth–Waterloo on 11 December 1982. The Waterloo–Exeter St Davids route is colloquially known as The Mule since it was downgraded from mainline status in the 1960s, due to the section of line from Salisbury to Exeter being something of a plod, but you'll get there.

Class 50s largely took over the Waterloo–Exeter St Davids route in 1980. By 1982, SR were not keen on unrefurbished Class 50s finding their way onto Waterloo services, as their poorer reliability could cause issues in case of failure, with long single-line sections west of Salisbury and the very busy commuter system east of Basingstoke. Sometimes unrefurbished examples still found their way onto The Mule though. Here we see 50026 *Indomitable* at Exeter St Davids backing down onto the 16.20 to Waterloo on 27 March 1982.

West of Salisbury, the ex-LSWR mainline ran through some beautiful and remote countryside. 50017 *Royal Oak* is hauling the 11.10 Waterloo–Exeter St Davids at Coker Wood, near the small hamlet of Pendomer, on 26 June 1983.

Having been audible for some minutes, 50020 *Revenge* echoes off the sides of the deep cutting at Cowdown Copse near Whitchurch as it climbs away from Hurstbourne viaduct. The train is the 05.45 Plymouth–Waterloo on 25 August 1982.

50007 *Hercules* rounds the curve at Whitford hauling the 11.10 Waterloo–Exeter St Davids on 30 August 1983. This locomotive spent less than a year in Large Logo livery from March 1983 until repainted into Brunswick Green in February 1984 for the GW150 celebrations.

The ex-LSWR mainline in Devon is a shadow of its former self when it was a direct competitor for the GWR. It is now single track for most of its length and is shorn of its branch lines. During the heyday of Class 50s on the route, 50021 *Rodney* is seen at Talaton with the 09.38 Exeter St Davids–Waterloo on 30 August 1983.

33022, near the village of Wilmington at Black Sand bridge, runs down the bank towards Seaton Junction with the 09.45 Exeter St Davids–Waterloo on 26 June 1983. Although generally replaced by Class 50s from 1980, use of Class 33s continued sporadically. The Brighton–Exeter service was diagrammed as such, double-headed on summer Saturdays.

50048 *Dauntless* is seen at Ammerham near Chard Junction with the 17.33 Exeter St Davids–Waterloo on 28 August 1986.

English Electric power on the LSWR mainline, but of a different generation to that normally seen. 40122/D200 blasts through Whitchurch with the front coach full of window hanging enthusiasts. This was a Ludgershall–Basingstoke working, part of the Basingstoke Rail Day event on 26 September 1987.

50027 *Lion* descends the bank at Milbourne Wick on the double-track Templecombe–Yeovil Junction section with the 13.10 Waterloo–Exeter St Davids on 6 August 1988. By this time the writing was on the wall for the Class 50s. Denied further main works overhauls, and subjected to a new component exchange maintenance regime they were not designed for, availability plunged. Class 47/4s were drafted in to help from October 1988, but they had smaller fuel tanks, which hampered flexibility; plus with the frequent station stops west of Salisbury, and the subsequent full power/full brake applications necessary to keep time, suffered from higher brake block wear, resulting in extra maintenance mid-diagram.

50018 *Resolution* coasts into Salisbury past the derelict water tower with the 10.15 from Waterloo on 19 January 1991. The remaining Hoovers were now taking on a rundown appearance; stand by one during a station stop, flaking paint and body corrosion were all too evident. From May 1989 a pool of twenty dedicated Class 50s was supposed to cover all Waterloo–Salisbury–Exeter diagrams, but in 1990 as few as six were available for traffic at times resulting in frequent substitutions, while from October 1990 several Class 33s reappeared on the route.

47701 *Old Oak Common Traction and Rolling Stock Depot* cruises towards Sherborne at Milbourne Wick on 24 May 1992 at the head of the 14.58 Waterloo–Exeter St Davids. Class 47/7s, which had larger fuel tanks, started appearing on loan during 1991, and by October that year were officially allocated to the line alongside the remaining Class 50s. Problems continued though, a result of using small pools of 25–30-year-old motive power on a route that was very demanding to work.

Although Class 50 operation officially ceased on 19 January 1992, in practise they still appeared occasionally on The Mule right up until 23 May 1992 when 50033 *Glorious* worked the 14.22 Exeter St Davids–Waterloo, unfortunately failing at Basingstoke with a main generator flashover. On Sunday 24 May 1992 D400/50050 (with its *Fearless* plates removed) and 50007 *Sir Edward Elgar* worked two round trips, double-headed, on public service trains between Exeter St Davids and Salisbury as a final farewell on the route. The pair are seen here passing the long-closed station at Dinton with the 09.28 Exeter St Davids–Waterloo.

50007 *Sir Edward Elgar* and D400/50050, complete with Farewell Class 50 headboard, pass Chicksgrove at the head of the final Class 50-hauled service train, the 17.00 Waterloo–Exeter St Davids, on 24 May 1992. These two Class 50s survived until 26 March 1994 working enthusiast railtours, but for me, this warm spring evening was the end.